Fast Asleep

Written by Gill Munton
Illustrated by Valeria Petrone

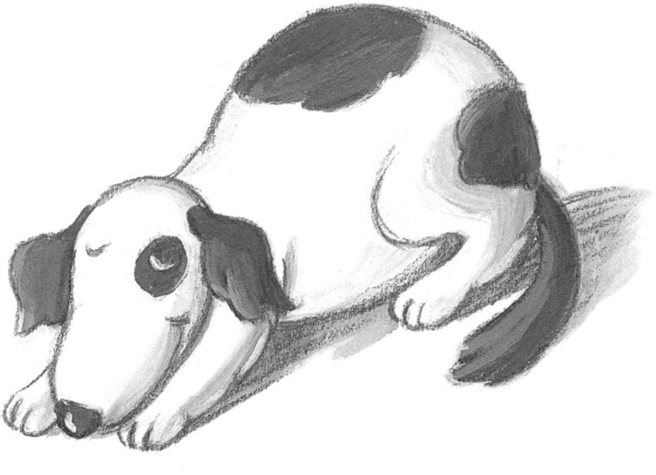

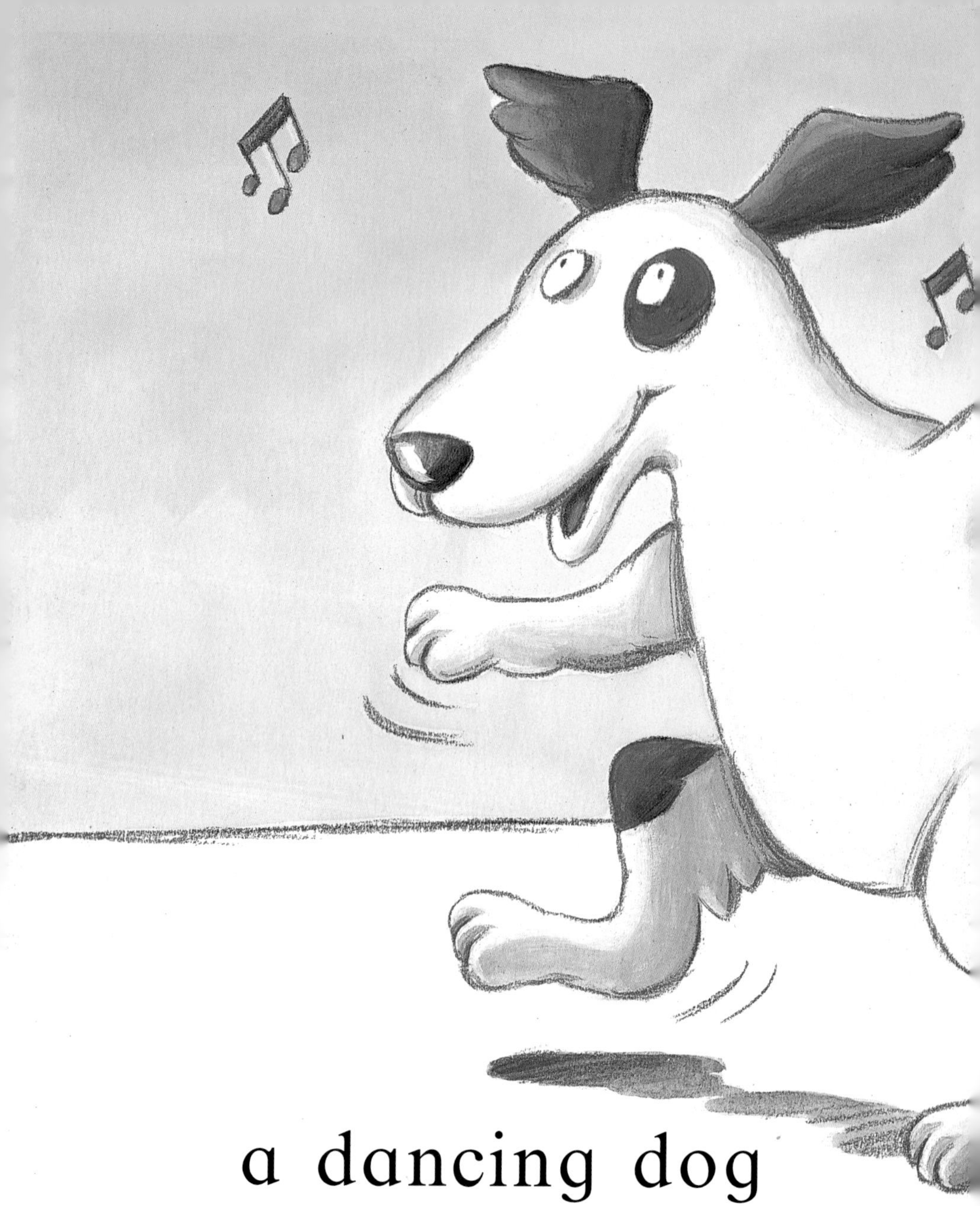

a dancing dog

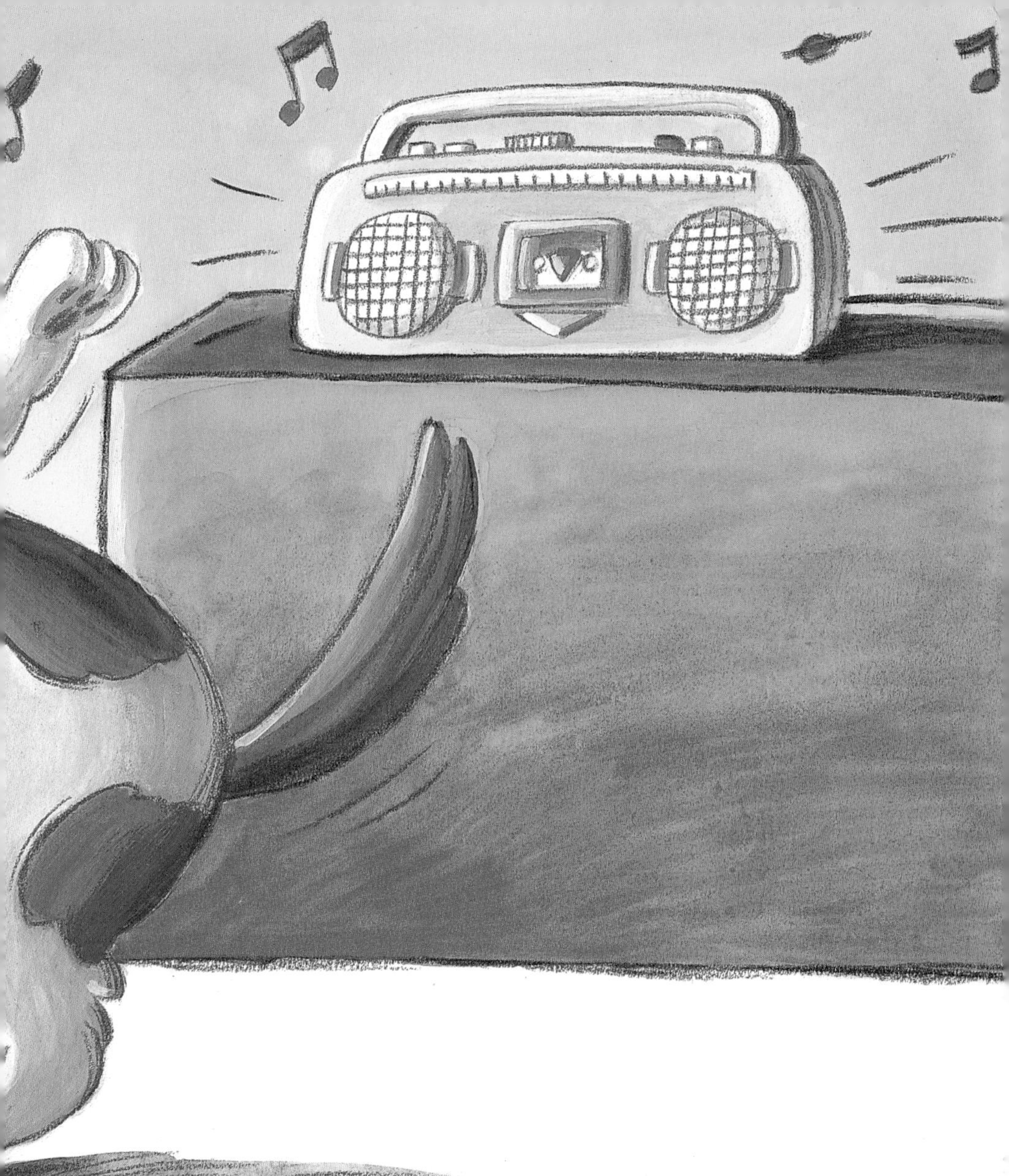

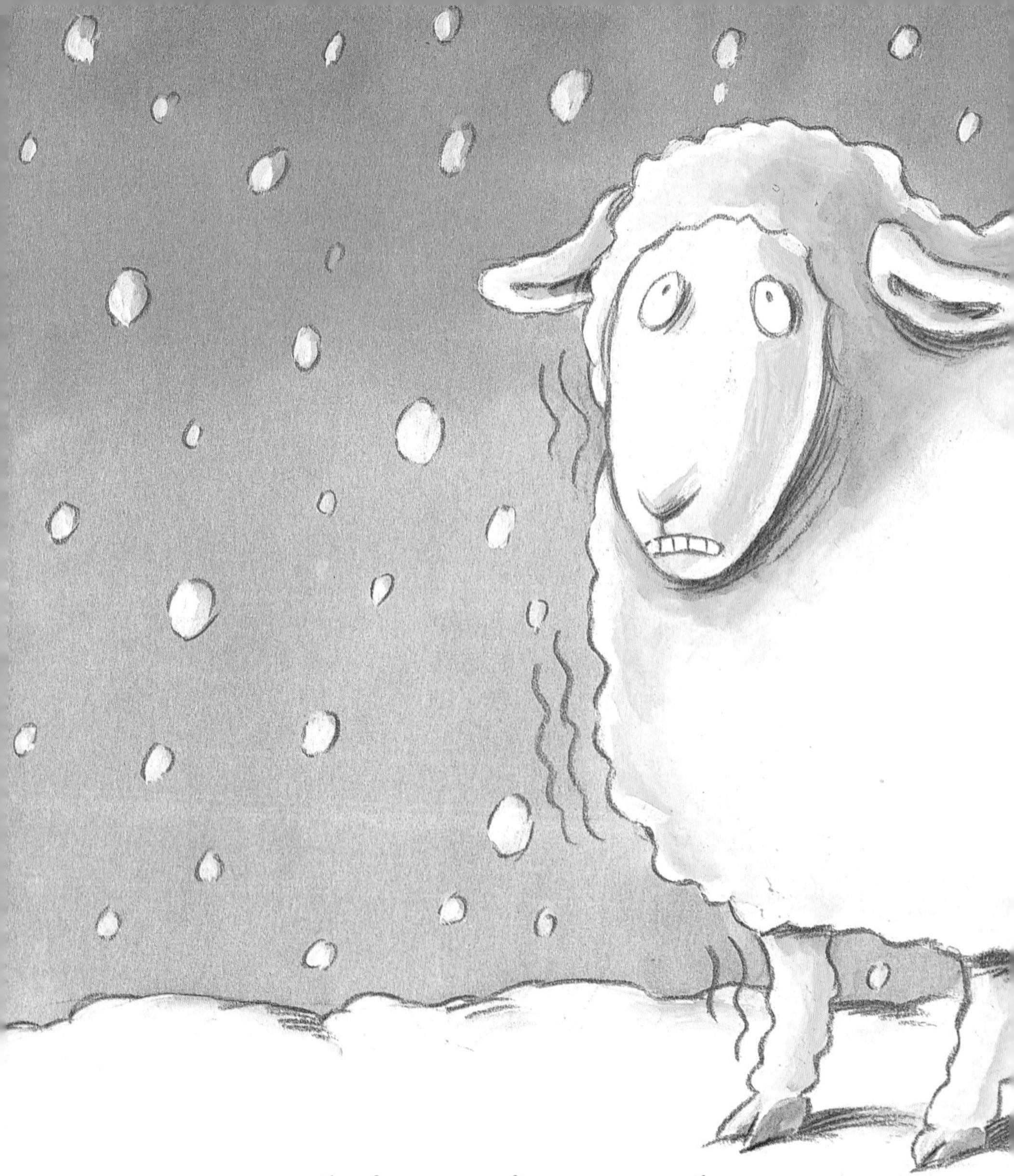

a shivering sheep

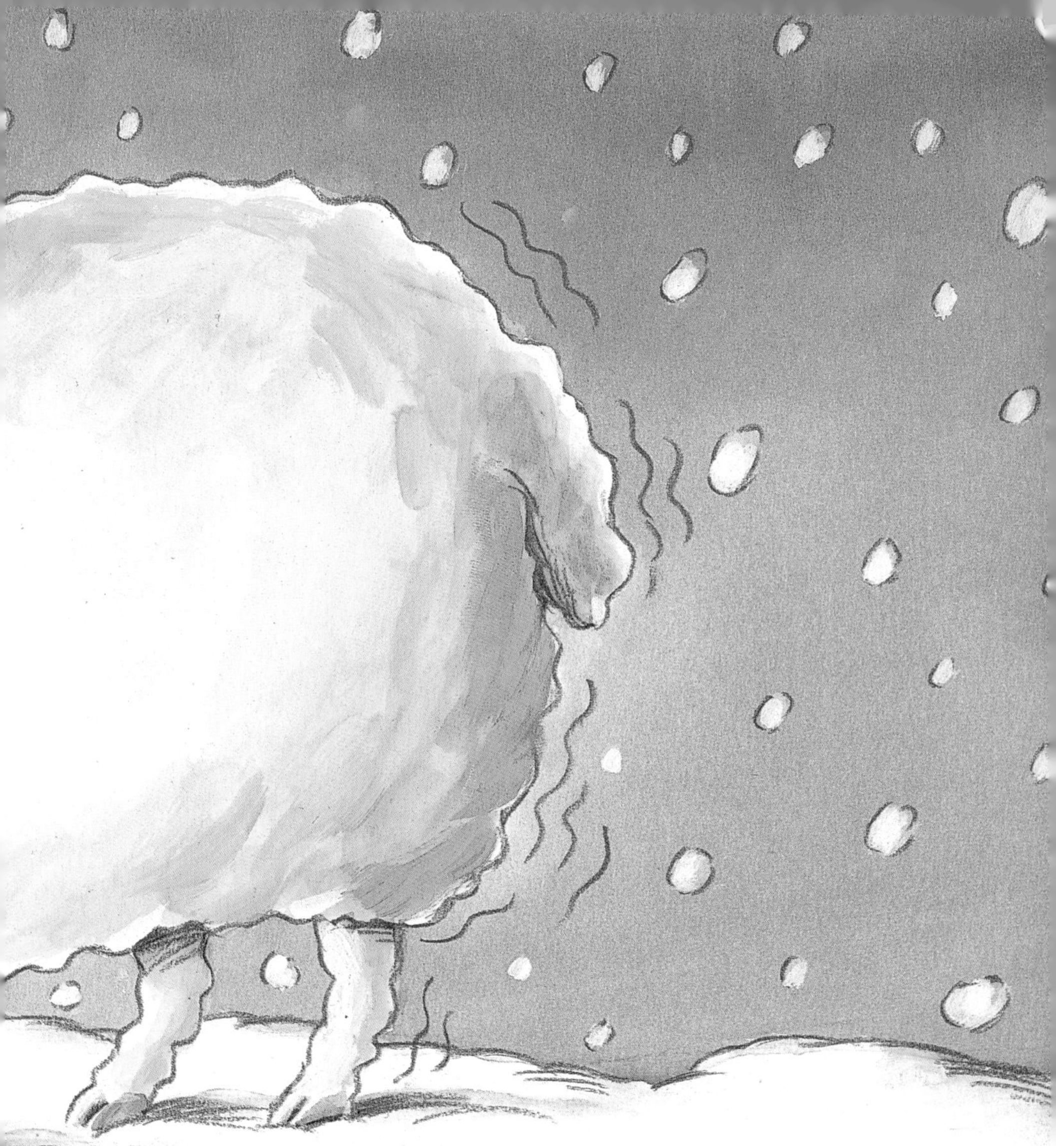

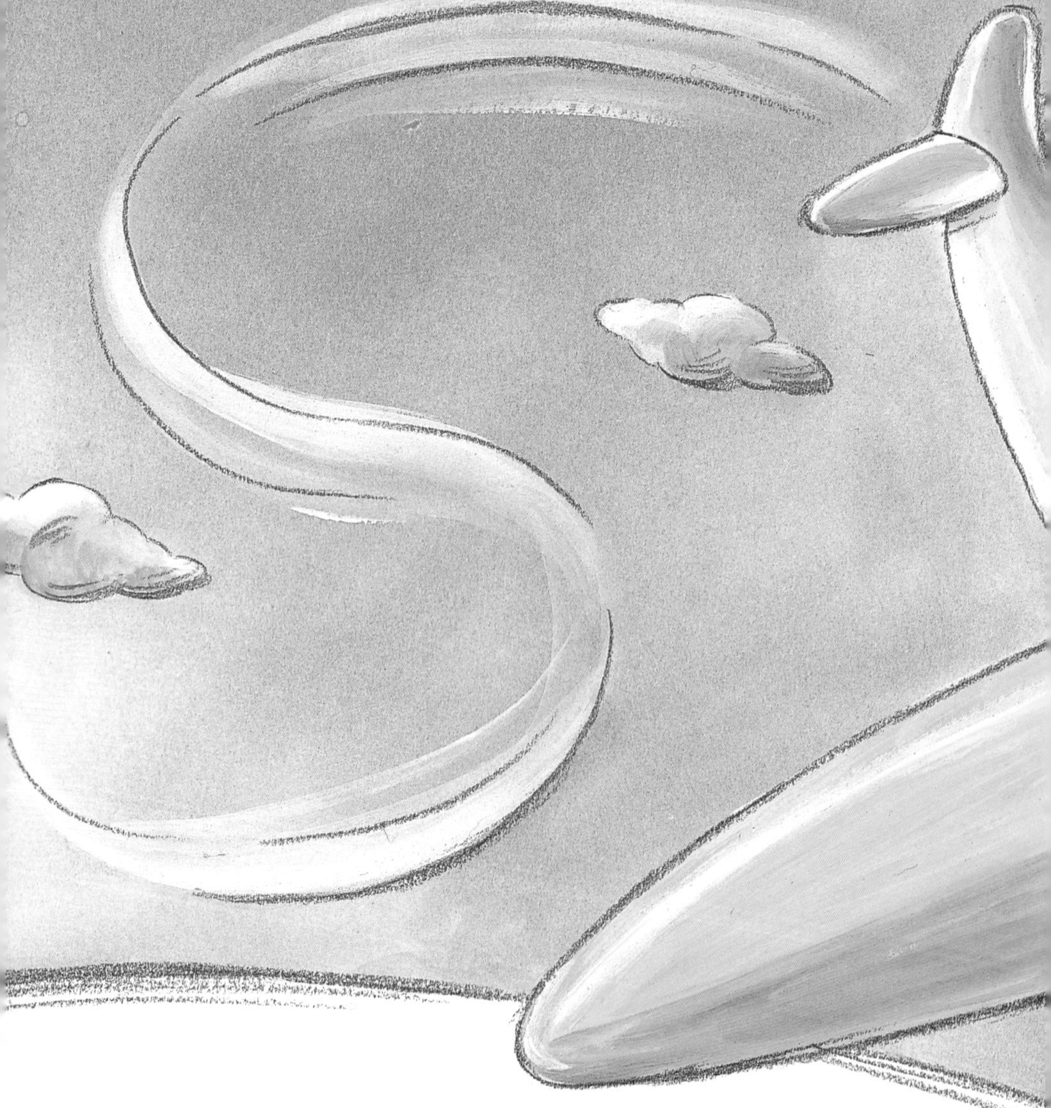

a flying frog

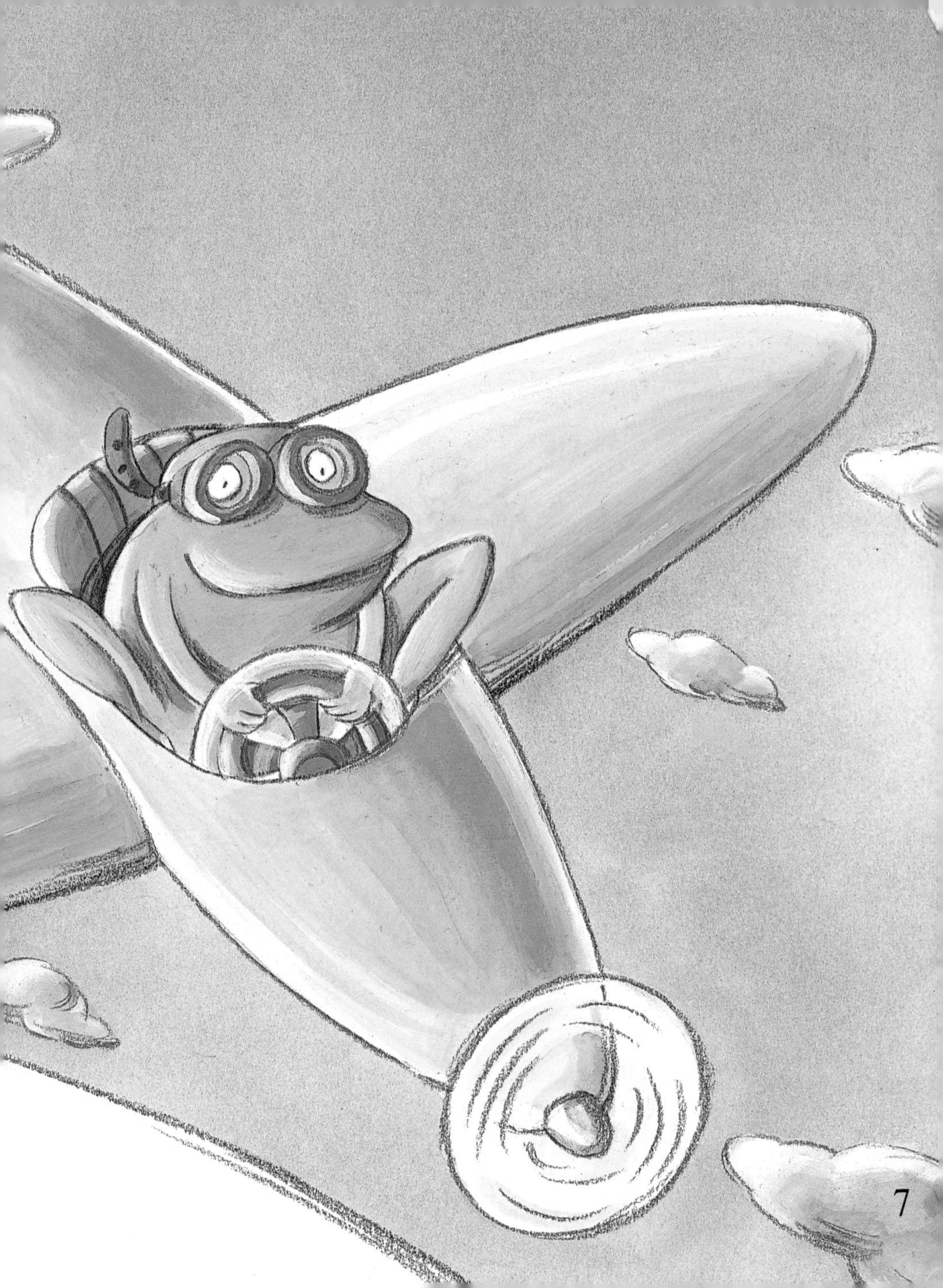

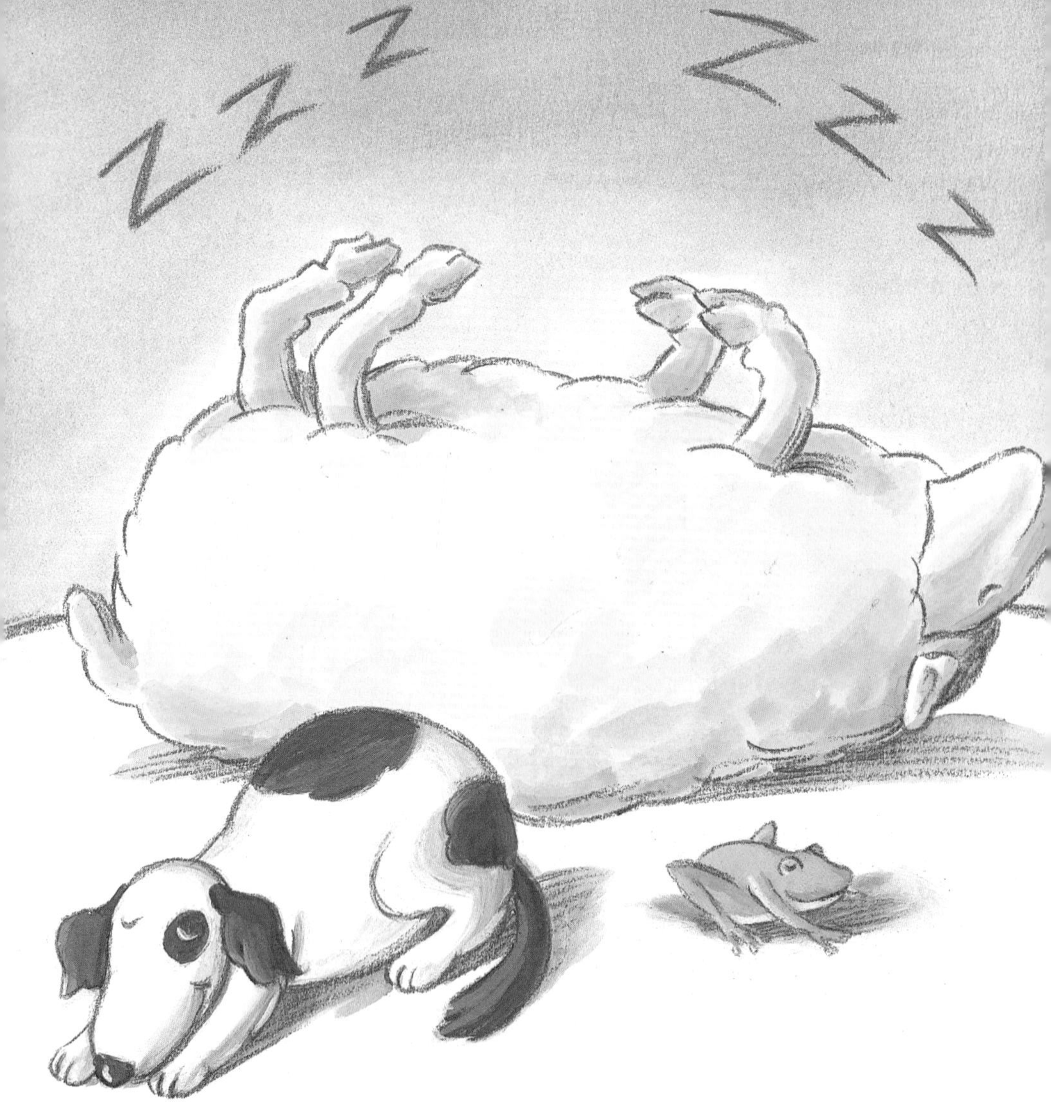

fast asleep